Managing Challenging People
dealing with staff conduct

Maureen Cooper & Bev Curtis

Published by Network Educational Press Ltd.
PO Box 635
Stafford
ST16 1BF

First Published 2000
© Maureen Cooper and Bev Curtis 2000

ISBN 1 85539 057 4

Maureen Cooper and Bev Curtis assert the right to be
identified as the authors of this work.

Every effort has been made to contact copyright holders
and the Publishers apologise for any omissions, which
they will be pleased to rectify at the earliest opportunity.

Series Co-ordinator · Anat Arkin
Series Editor · Carol Etherington
Cover design by Neil Hawkins, Devine Design
Internal design and layout by Neil Gordon, Init Publishing
Illustrations by Barking Dog Art

Printed in Great Britain by
Redwood Books, Trowbridge, Wilts.

CONTENTS

INTRODUCTION

The overwhelming majority of people who work in schools are highly professional in their approach to pupils, colleagues and other members of the school community. There are, however, those whose attitudes or conduct pose a challenge to headteachers and other senior managers in schools. Both teaching and non-teaching staff can occasionally be difficult to manage.

Dealing with these individuals successfully is largely a question of adopting an appropriate management style. School managers need to be fair and consistent and, wherever possible, involve staff in decision-making - but they should not shy away from the difficult task of challenging those whose conduct falls short of expectations.

In this handbook, we examine the role of school managers in dealing with different kinds of misconduct. We also consider the legal context in which school disciplinary procedures have to be seen, and give practical advice on implementing these procedures. Case studies drawn from our experience of working with primary and secondary schools are used throughout the book. Model documents and procedures, which readers may wish to adapt for use in their own schools, are also provided. We are grateful to Cambridgeshire LEA for permission to use their Disciplinary Rules and Disciplinary Procedure for Misconduct (see Appendices A and B).

Like other handbooks in the Education Personnel Management series, *Managing Challenging People* is aimed primarily at senior managers in schools and members of the Governing Body's staffing committee. A short summary of the role of governors in managing challenging staff is included for the benefit of other governors.

Maureen Cooper and Bev Curtis

The following icons are used throughout the book to identify certain types of information:

Case Study

Legal

Checklist

Model Procedure

CHAPTER 1
THE MANAGEMENT CHALLENGE

Management styles

It goes without saying that headteachers and other school managers need to be fair, reasonable and consistent in their approach to those they manage. A bullying management style will demotivate staff and is likely to destroy the goodwill that exists in the school.

Headteachers do, however, need to be prepared to manage staff and let them know what is expected of them. Managers in private industry usually recognise that the management of people is one of their primary functions. In education, on the other hand, many senior staff see their role primarily in terms of managing the curriculum, rather than the people who deliver that curriculum and carry out the many other tasks associated with the life of a school. Despite the growing emphasis on target setting and on monitoring and evaluating performance, the management of staff is, paradoxically, given a very low priority in many schools.

Yet senior managers, like other teachers, have well developed people-management skills that they routinely use when dealing with pupils. Few competent teachers would let pupils get away with repeated lateness or disruptive behaviour. They would see it as their job to do all they could to change such behaviour. The principles for dealing with staff are not all that different: challenging staff, like challenging pupils, need to be treated fairly but also firmly and consistently.

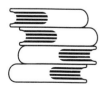

A routine problem

If a pupil refused to do his or her homework, giving various excuses ranging from "The dog ate my work" to "I couldn't understand it", as the class teacher, what would you do?

As soon as you became aware of the problem, you would probably take the pupil to one side and try to find out if something was troubling them.

If it turned out that other children had been bullying him or her for being a 'swot' or that a part-time job was taking up too much of their time, you might take practical steps to tackle these problems. If, however, the pupil was simply being lazy, you would probably give him or her a stern pep talk and perhaps set targets or use other measures to make sure the homework got done. You would then keep a close eye on the pupil's performance.

Dealing with a teacher who, for example, refuses to comply with the school's marking policy requires essentially the same approach, namely:

- challenge the unacceptable behaviour as soon as you become aware of it;
- establish its cause;
- if it is deliberate recalcitrance, warn the teacher that it must not continue;
- monitor the situation for a set period of time.

The reluctance of many school managers to tell staff what they are required to do and how they are expected to act may be a legacy of the days when responsibility for staff management lay largely with local education authorities. In our experience, such reluctance is certainly far more widespread than bullying and harassing management behaviour, though its effects on the well-being of a school and its pupils can be just as damaging. Managers who are faced with staff whose conduct or attitude is a cause for concern should therefore be prepared to exercise their authority, engage in conversations that are bound to be difficult and take whatever further measures may be necessary.

Of course, there has to be some give and take. No school would want to run with a staff of clones, and managers have to recognise that schools, like other organisations, have their fair share of colourful individuals and eccentrics! There are also bound to be differences in approach; for example an English department might develop a very different ethos from that of the science department in the same school. So, an element of flexibility needs to be set against the need for consistent standards of behaviour.

This requires school managers to make some very fine judgements. For example, headteachers may be inclined to take a fairly relaxed view of a charismatic member of staff who, while sometimes turning up late to classes, also manages to achieve good results. If, however, a less successful teacher were to behave in the same way, the head may well be inclined to be far less lenient. Managers need to set clear standards of conduct and apply these consistently.

The causes of challenging conduct

People do not usually become unreliable, dishonest or just plain awkward overnight. In the rare cases where there is a sudden change in an individual's behaviour, managers need to find out why this has happened. Is it the result of pressures or problems at work or is it to do with personal circumstances? Sometimes an over-assertive or aggressive response to a situation is a clear indication that things have gone wrong in an employee's personal life and, where this is the case, management needs to respond sympathetically to what may be a temporary aberration.

More often, however, people become difficult gradually because no-one ever comments on their attitude or approach or the way they conduct themselves. In other words, where a member of staff has long behaved in ways that are inconsistent with a school's expectations, there are usually two problems, not one. There is the problem of the individual's conduct and there is a failure on the part of the management to deal with that conduct.

As well as challenging staff whose conduct has become unacceptable, there is much that headteachers and other senior managers can do to prevent such problems occurring in the future.

The recruitment process obviously plays a key part in ensuring that the right people are employed to work in a school. If a significant proportion of recently appointed staff are under-performing or behaving in ways that are unacceptable, there is clearly something seriously wrong with the school's selection methods.

Overhauling these methods may not, however, be enough to ensure that new members of staff fulfil their responsibilities in the way that the school expects. Induction is equally important in this respect, yet many management textbooks will go into great detail about recruitment and selection procedures but say very little about the induction period. The Government now requires all schools to address the very specific induction needs of newly-qualified teachers, but other members of staff joining a school also need support and guidance. It is crucial that experienced teachers, especially those appointed to management posts, are guided in the way that the school wishes them to fulfil their responsibilities.

Similarly, non-teaching staff need to be inducted into the ways of the school and learn how they are expected to deal with pupils, parents and other members of staff. The lunch-time supervisor who is rude to children and the school secretary who is offhand with callers are often able to argue, with some justification, that no-one has told them that these forms of behaviour are unacceptable.

Staff recruitment and selection and induction are examined in more detail in another handbook in this series.

Promoting professional conduct: a checklist for school managers

- Do all senior members of staff recognise that the management of people forms a key part of their role?
- Have the school's selection processes been reviewed recently to ensure that the right people are appointed to every post?
- Does the school set clear standards of conduct? Do managers apply these standards consistently?
- Do the school's induction processes ensure that all teaching and non-teaching staff know how they are expected to act?
- Is unacceptable behaviour always challenged promptly?

Management problems for the newly-appointed headteacher

Inheriting a school where particular patterns of staff behaviour have been allowed to develop, sometimes over many years, is probably one of the most difficult management situations that any headteacher has to face.

The advice often given to newly-appointed heads is to spend their first few months in post familiarising themselves with the school, its staff and its culture before introducing any change. Like the curate's egg, this advice is good in parts.

From an employment law perspective, it is important that the new headteacher does not leave inappropriate conduct unchallenged. If such conduct should eventually lead to dismissal, and perhaps to a claim for unfair dismissal, one of the questions that an employment tribunal will ask is when the headteacher first began addressing the perceived problem. If the head has waited for two, three or more terms before taking any action, the tribunal may draw the inference that the conduct of the employee concerned could not have been all that objectionable or it would not have been allowed to continue for so long.

Also, from a common sense point of view, staff might reasonably believe that everything was satisfactory if no-one has ever said anything to them to the contrary. So, as a rule of thumb, the more serious a problem appears to be, the more quickly it should be dealt with.

When challenged, established members of staff may sometimes argue that it is the new headteacher who has got things wrong, since no-one has ever complained about their behaviour before. Arguments of this kind should not be allowed to deter the headteacher from managing difficult staff. In fact, where it is just one individual who is awkward or unco-operative, a new head may gain the respect of other colleagues by dealing with this behaviour promptly.

The problem is more difficult to manage if unacceptable patterns of behaviour have become deeply entrenched among a group of staff. In these situations, the headteacher will feel isolated and will need considerable support from governors, external inspectors and advisers. If that support is not forthcoming, the head may eventually find the problems insurmountable and may be the one who leaves the school first.

Clockwatchers

A new headteacher was appointed to a school where there had been little staff turnover for many years. Under the previous head, the school's somewhat relaxed culture had become entrenched. Teachers expected to work only from 9 a.m. to 3.45 p.m. each day, and, in order to make sure they could leave at the same time as pupils, staff meetings were always held during the lunch break.

The new head felt this was not the most efficient way of dealing with all the demands of contemporary school life. Soon after his appointment, he announced that in future most meetings would be held after school, even if that meant that on occasion people would have to stay until five o'clock.

Despite a certain amount of grumbling, the great majority of staff turned up at the later meetings.

The one notable exception was a long-serving history teacher who was the representative of one of the teacher unions at the school. He complained about the bureaucratic burden the new head was imposing on staff, and supported his case with a union policy document which stated that teachers should not be expected to attend more than one meeting of up to an hour's duration per week.

When this union representative refused to attend the second of two meetings held in one week, and unsuccessfully incited colleagues to do the same, the headteacher realised he could not leave this conduct unchallenged. As a first step, he refreshed his memory of the teachers' pay and conditions document, which clearly states that, contractually, a full-time time teacher is required to "be available to perform such duties at such times and such places as may be specified by the headteacher...for 1,265 hours in any school year, those hours to be allocated reasonably throughout those days in the school year on which he is required to be available for work."

Armed with this information, and confident that he was on firm ground, the headteacher was able to point out to the union representative that his refusal to attend more than one meeting per week was a breach of his contract of employment. The conversation that they had was not an easy one, but it enabled the head to resolve the immediate problem without resorting to formal disciplinary action. It took much longer, of course, to change the culture of the school.

CHAPTER 2
HANDLING DIFFERENT
KINDS OF MISCONDUCT

Staff attitudes

Apparently unco-operative behaviour sometimes reflects a lack of training. We have already mentioned the importance of the induction period, but the need to provide training does not end there. Take, for example, a caretaker who fails to use the right equipment when carrying out maintenance work and endangers his own and other people's safety. In order to prove that this is wilful misconduct, management would have to show that the caretaker had received the appropriate training or instructions.

Rudeness and plain awkwardness can also sometimes be tackled through training. Short courses in communication skills or customer care are now widely available and may lead to improvements in the way employees deal with colleagues, pupils and visitors to the school.

Insubordination is a harder nut to crack, and formal disciplinary action may be the only way to deal with individuals who refuse to accept managers' authority.

Dishonesty

Dishonesty can be found in all walks of life, and schools are no exception. Disciplinary rules should make it clear that theft, even of minor items such as toilet rolls or light bulbs, is unacceptable.

Managers should also make sure that staff whose jobs involve handling money are properly trained and supervised, and that financial procedures are always followed.

Missing funds

When things got too much for the school secretary of a small primary school, she began taking the dinner money home to count it. The months passed and she did not get around to bringing it back. Eventually, bags and bags of money were discovered in her home, none of it actually missing.

This was clearly not a case of deliberate dishonesty. The secretary's actions were the result of a management failure both to recognise the signs of work overload and to follow proper accounting procedures.

Nevertheless, issues of this kind should be dealt with under a school's disciplinary procedure, since the proverbial man or woman on the Clapham omnibus would probably say that the secretary's behaviour, whatever its causes, was unacceptable. Doing nothing about it would set an unfortunate precedent, although the school secretary should not have to shoulder all the blame. It would also be reasonable to take disciplinary action against those who had neglected to manage her properly.

Harassment

Managers dealing with allegations of harassment need to focus on the effect this behaviour is having on the person at the receiving end, rather than on the intention of the perpetrator, who will often respond in astonishment when challenged about his or her behaviour. It is particularly important to consider allegations of harassment from the recipient's point of view in cases of sexual harassment.

Sometimes harassment starts as a 'joke' or seemingly innocent light-hearted behaviour. Whilst initially this may be acceptable, it can become unacceptable if it persists. Harassers often fail to appreciate the change in their colleague's attitude, and unless they are challenged, will argue - quite reasonably - that their own behaviour has not changed. They need to be told that what they are doing is no longer acceptable.

13

A harassment checklist

Harassment can take many forms, including:

- visual displays - for example posters, graffiti, photographs, indecent exposure, obscene gestures, flags and emblems;

- verbal harassment - for example rudeness, name calling and personal remarks;

- unwanted physical approaches - for example touching, feeling, stroking, leering, staring, assault and violence;

- isolation, exclusion or compulsion - for example unfair allocation of work, compulsion to or exclusion from taking part in certain activities;

- surveillance and intrusion - for example following, lingering, pestering and deliberate obstruction, all of which may continue outside the workplace; interfering with and defacing personal possessions or property.

Once an employee has made it clear to the harasser, or to a manager, that a certain type of behaviour causes offence, repetition of that behaviour may well be held by an employment tribunal to amount to harassment.

Unwelcomed advances

Ms Bell, a young female English teacher, joined High Hill School this term and has been to see the deputy head alleging that her head of department, Mr Clarke, is making unwanted advances to her, which she claims amount to sexual harassment. Mr Clarke has a reputation in the school for 'helping' young female members of his department rather more than anyone else. Ms Bell says he has written poems to her, taken her to the theatre on the pretext of developing her understanding of drama and kissed her on the cheek in the taxi on the way home. She finds it very difficult to tell him to stop behaving in this way because he is her boss and responsible for her induction programme.

A case of this kind should be dealt with as a disciplinary issue, and illustrates why every school needs to have a harassment policy. Allegations of harassment need to be handled promptly, sensitively and firmly, preferably by someone of the same sex as the complainant. Cases that are serious should lead to disciplinary action, but many can be resolved by a well-trained, sensitive manager without resorting to such a damaging and necessarily public outcome.

Senior managers need to recognise that the person on the receiving end of unwanted attention or overbearing conduct may feel too embarrassed or intimidated to handle the matter personally. Since the school is legally responsible for its employees' actions in these situations, a senior manager should make it clear to the offending member of staff that what he or she is doing is causing offence, and set out in writing what needs to be done to put things right.

Sometimes managers are tempted to move the complainant to another area of the school or make timetable changes to prevent the two parties from meeting. While it be may be sensible to try to minimise contact, case law has established that moving a victim of harassment, rather than the harasser, can itself amount to discrimination and/or victimisation.

The legal position

An employee can make a complaint to an employment tribunal of sexual or racial harassment. The definition of 'victimisation' in the 1975 Sex Discrimination Act includes treating a man or a woman less favourably than a member of the other sex on the grounds that he or she has complained of sex discrimination. There is a similar definition of victimisation in the 1976 Race Relations Act.

An employee who shows that harassment has occurred and that it would not have occurred to a member of the opposition sex or to someone from a different racial group is likely to have a strong case. The test a tribunal will apply is whether the individual concerned experienced hurt or outrage.

One of the reasons why growing numbers of employees in all occupations are exercising this right may be because there is no limit to the amount of compensation that a tribunal may award a successful complainant.

> In a school, it is the Governing Body that is 'vicariously liable' for the discriminatory acts of employees committed with or without the governors' knowledge or approval. Case law has established that even a single incident, provided that it is sufficiently serious, will constitute harassment and leave both the harasser and the Governing Body liable if the harasser is found to have "acted during the course of his or her employment".

If a case reaches an employment tribunal, the Governing Body will be required to show that it took reasonably practicable steps to prevent discriminatory acts occurring or reoccurring. The existence of a school policy on discrimination and harassment, supported by guidelines and training, would help to demonstrate that preventative measures had been taken.

Work-life balance

With a large proportion of the workforce now combining work with family commitments, managers need to be sensitive to the needs of employees who have childcare or other responsibilities. Ignoring these needs can lead to the loss of valued staff.

This does not mean, however, that the life of a school should revolve around the convenience of a few individuals. While it is quite reasonable for a teacher with young children or elderly dependent parents to negotiate a part-time contract, demanding a timetable that requires attendance in school only on Wednesdays and Thursdays, for example, is another matter. Staff who manage to carve things out to their own advantage and to the disadvantage of colleagues can cause ill feeling, and need to be dealt with in the same way as anyone else whose attitude to work is a cause of concern.

Having said that, managers need to appreciate that, where a woman who has been on maternity leave asks to return to work on a part-time or job-share basis, refusal can amount to indirect sex discrimination. The following employment tribunal case illustrates this potential pitfall.

Job share

A pregnant infant school teacher asked her headteacher if she could job-share when she returned from maternity leave. Another teacher employed on a temporary contract at the school was interested in the job-share and the two had discussed how they might divide the work.

The governors of the school turned down the application. Unable to return to full-time teaching because she could not find a nursery place for her new-born baby near her home, the teacher resigned. She had not known until her application was rejected that the local education authority had a job-sharing scheme based on the principle that all full-time teaching posts could be filled on a job-sharing basis.

The headteacher of the school was also unaware of the LEA's scheme, but when she found out about it, failed to tell the teacher concerned - an omission that, according to the employment tribunal, struck at the heart of the relationship of trust and confidence implicit in all employment contracts.

The tribunal found that the teacher had been constructively and unfairly dismissed. It also found that the Governing Body of the school and the LEA had discriminated against her under the Sex Discrimination Act by requiring her to work full-time. Although this requirement would have applied equally to a man, the fact that a much smaller proportion of women than men were able to comply with it amounted to indirect sex discrimination.

The decision might have gone in favour of the governors and the LEA if they had managed to justify the rejection of the job-share application on objective grounds. However, the tribunal held that the headteacher's view that a job-share would create practical problems was a subjective one.

Dress and appearance

Individuals' dress and appearance are sensitive matters, and the introduction of a dress code for staff should be handled carefully. However, whether they like it or not, staff in schools, particularly teachers, are role models for pupils. They are also ambassadors for the school whenever they come into contact with parents or attend external meetings or other functions on behalf of the school. Many people would take the view that it is indefensible to chastise pupils for turning up at school bedraggled or out of uniform if staff get way with a scruffy and unkempt appearance. School managers are therefore quite within their rights to insist that employees conform to certain standards of smartness.

In relation to women staff, the most common complaints are do with 'provocative' dress and inappropriate jewellery or make up. With men, the problem is more commonly scruffiness or a refusal to wear a jacket or tie. Occasionally, with either sex, there are concerns about the delicate question of personal hygiene or the wearing of political badges or insignia.

Subjecting an employee of one sex to a rule which is not applicable to members of the other sex could amount to unlawful sex discrimination. An example would be where women are allowed to wear jewellery at work but men are not, or where women are forbidden from wearing trousers or men from having long hair.

However, according to the decision in *Smith v Safety plc* (1996) IRLR 456 CA, employers can legitimately maintain different dress and appearance codes for men and women, provided that they do have a code for both sexes and enforce a common standard of smartness and conventionality. The court held that in this case the employer was acting fairly in denying a male employee the right to attend work with his hair in a pony tail, even though there was no rule preventing a female employee from doing so. Similarly, in *Kara v London Borough of Hackney* (1995) 325/95 EAT, a male employee failed in his attempt to prove unlawful sex discrimination when he was prevented from wearing a skirt at work, even though women employees could wear trousers.

Any code relating to dress and appearance should be reasonable and Governing Bodies should seek to reach agreement with staff and their representatives before introducing it. Where agreement is not reached, and the Governing Body is satisfied that the code is reasonable, it would be well advised to give a term's notice before introducing the code.

Dress and appearance codes may affect some employees more than others because of their racial or cultural origins or religious beliefs. If individuals object to a code on these grounds, the governors must be able to justify the need for particular rules.

Where a school has a dress code, it is important that it is applied consistently. If some employees are challenged about their appearance while others are allowed to dress as they please, this could give rise to claims of unfairness and victimisation. This is particularly the case where the employee believes that the inconsistent treatment is related to his or her race, culture or religion.

The consequences of breaking rules relating to dress and appearance should be made clear to all staff. They should be aware that if informal attempts to resolve the problem fail, then formal disciplinary action may be used.

A sartorial challenge

Peter Bennett has been teaching in a small village primary school for 10 years. A new head, Mrs Granger, has recently been appointed following a long period of disruption when the previous head was on sick leave and the deputy, a good friend of Peter's, was acting head.

Mrs Granger soon discovers that Peter is charming but 'shambolic', especially in his appearance. Comments from parents include the following:

"The children have to tuck their shirts in, but apparently Mr Bennett doesn't have to."

"How can I get my son to smarten up when his teacher looks such a mess?"

"My daughter says she'll do Mr Bennett's homework when he cleans his shoes."

Mrs Granger has decided that she needs to tackle Peter about his appearance.

How should she address this problem?

First, she should invite Peter to a meeting, where she should point out what parents have been saying and set out some guidelines as to what she expects from staff.

Ideally, Mrs Granger should tell Peter a day or so in advance that she wants to meet him to discuss his appearance. This will ensure that Peter cannot complain that the meeting has been sprung on him without warning. Rather than sending him a memo 'out of the blue', she should invite him to the meeting in person, and describe it as a 'professional discussion' or use some other term that makes it clear that, while this is not a formal disciplinary meeting, it is more than just a chat. If, on being invited to the meeting, Peter tries to have the discussion there and then, perhaps by asking what is wrong with his appearance, Mrs Granger should say something along the lines of: "We will have a full discussion about this on Friday - but not now".

She might then send him a note confirming the meeting. Although there is, of course, no entitlement for an employee to be accompanied at a management discussion, Mrs Granger could let Peter bring a 'friend' along if she felt that this person would be likely to counsel him behind the scenes to smarten himself up.

To: **Peter Bennett**
From: **Sheila Granger**
Re: **Professional discussion**

As I indicated to you this morning, I would like to meet you on Friday at 3.15 p.m. to discuss some concerns that I have about the image you are presenting to pupils, parents and colleagues.

This meeting is not of a formal disciplinary nature, so there is no entitlement for you to be accompanied, but you may, exceptionally, bring a trade union representative or friend with you if you feel this would be helpful. If you decide to do so, please let me know before the meeting.

During the meeting, Mrs Granger should avoid arguing with Peter and stick firmly, but not aggressively, to the points she wishes to raise. She should let Peter respond and take a note of his main points. However, she should make sure she remains in charge of the meeting and say she wants to move on to the next point once Peter has had a reasonable opportunity to have his say.

Some managers find it useful to prepare for professional discussions by writing down the points they wish to raise in the form of a 'script'. This should outline the purpose of the discussion, refer specifically to each concern and indicate why it is a concern, set targets for improvement and give a review date. By allowing for the employee's response to each point that is raised, the script can later be used as a record of the discussion.

We are not suggesting that a manager should slavishly read out every word in such a script. However, the process of preparing a script can help to clarify the objectives of a professional discussion. By referring to it in the course of the meeting, the manager can also ensure that the discussion remains within his or her control.

Meeting with Peter Bennett

1. Outline the purpose of the meeting
"Peter, as you know, the purpose of this meeting is to discuss with you some concerns I have about the image you are presenting."

2. Be specific about each concern and indicate why it is a concern
"I'm afraid I have to tell you that you look untidy and dishevelled and really do not present an appropriate role model for the children, particularly when we place a lot of emphasis on the children being dressed appropriately."

3. Allow a response to each concern that has been raised
Let Peter respond and take a note of his comments. Then say: "I'd like to move on to the next point now."

4. Set targets
"Peter, I strongly advise you that you make sure you always look clean and tidy when you are at school or representing the school. For example, your shoes should be cleaned and your shirt should be done up, even on a hot day."

5. Set a review date
"I'd like to meet you again to review the position at the end of term. At that time, I want to be able to say that there is no longer a problem."

Alcohol use and abuse

Teachers and other school employees, like all adults, are entitled to have a drink at lunch-time or after school. What they do in their own time is their own business, unless it impairs their ability to do their job or brings the school's good name into disrepute.

Sometimes, it is only when an employee's work performance begins to suffer that it becomes apparent that he or she has a drink problem. Alcohol abusers often go to great lengths to conceal their problem, and overt drunkenness is rare in the workplace. Managers need to watch out for more subtle signs such as odd behaviour after lunch or the smell of drink on an employee's breath.

Alcohol abuse may be symptomatic of a health problem, in which case the employee concerned should be referred to counselling and, if that does not help, should be dealt with under the school's competency procedure. (We return to this point later in the book.)

Where there is no evidence of a health problem, drunkenness becomes a disciplinary issue. An employee who, for example, becomes loud and aggressive after having 'one too many' will need to handled in the same way as the sartorially challenged teacher in the above case study.

Staff discipline and grievance procedures

When challenged about unacceptable behaviour, staff will sometimes respond by accusing management of bullying them. Some will also try to bypass disciplinary proceedings by starting grievance proceedings of their own. On no account should this be allowed. Instead, any counter charge the employee wishes to make should be raised under the school's disciplinary procedure. Procedural matters and their legal background are discussed in the following chapters.

CHAPTER 3
THE LEGAL BACKGROUND

From an employment law perspective, managing people in schools is more complex than managing people in other organisations. This is because the employment of staff in schools is governed by two distinct sets of laws. Employment law, which is enshrined in Acts of Parliament, European Union directives and case law, applies to all employers. In addition, governors and senior managers in schools have to take account of a further raft of education law, which affects the management of employees.

Employment law

Recent legislation has significantly strengthened employees' rights to fair treatment in the workplace. The Employment Relations Act 1999 raised the upper limit for compensation for unfair dismissal from £12,000 to £50,000, while also reducing the qualifying period for protection from unfair dismissal from two years to one. This means that whereas some schools might, in the past, have used one-year, fixed-term contracts as an unofficial 'probationary period' for new members of staff, they are now likely to face an unfair dismissal claim unless they have a good reason for refusing to renew an employee's one-year contract.

Dismissals checklist

Employment law recognises just five fair reasons for dismissal:

- conduct;
- capability;
- statutory enactment;
- redundancy;
- some other substantial reason.

'Statutory enactment' covers those situations where an employer cannot legally continue to employ an individual. An example is the dismissal of a newly-qualified teacher who has failed to complete the statutory induction period satisfactorily. In such a case, the governors cannot legally continue to employ the teacher, who would have to be dismissed on the grounds of statutory enactment.

Dismissal for 'some other substantial reason' is the category into which a number of other types of dismissals fit, but the reason does have to be a substantial one. A situation where governors have lost all confidence in the headteacher's ability to lead the school might fall into this category.

Dismissal on grounds of ill health, should it come before an employment tribunal, would most often come under the heading of 'capability'. However, a recent case demonstrates that sometimes it might be a case of dismissal for 'some other substantial reason'. If ill health becomes an issue in a conduct case, it needs to be dealt with separately and in an appropriate way. Detailed guidelines on dealing with issues of staff health are provided in *The Well Teacher*, another handbook in the Education Personnel Management series.

While senior managers in schools need to be aware of these key aspects of employment protection legislation, they do not normally have the time to turn themselves into experts on employment law. Nor is it necessary to refer to the legal framework to obtain guidance about good practice. One of the best sources of advice on employment law comes from the Advisory Conciliation and Arbitration Service (ACAS), which has produced a range of handbooks and issues a code of practice, which includes guidance on the essential features of disciplinary procedures.

The ACAS code does not have the force of law. Its status is similar to that of the Highway Code, in that if you ignore one of the rules in the Highway Code, the chances are that somewhere along the line you have acted without regard to the law. Similarly, an employer who fails to follow ACAS advice has probably fallen foul of some aspect of employment law because it could be held that he or she has acted unreasonably.

Education law

The most important piece of current education legislation in relation to managing staff is the School Standards and Framework Act 1998, which incorporates many of the principles laid down in earlier legislation. The Act gives Governing Bodies of maintained schools full responsibility for managing teaching and non-teaching staff whose salaries come out of the school's budget. It also gives school employees the right to make representations at dismissal hearings and to appeal against dismissal.

The School Standards and Framework Act 1998: key elements

Discipline

Schedule 16 of the Act, which applies to community, voluntary controlled and community special schools, includes the following provision (in paragraph 22).

"The regulation of conduct and discipline in relation to the staff of the school, and any procedures for giving members of the staff opportunities for seeking redress of any grievances relating to their employment, shall be under the control of the Governing Body."

The Act goes on to say that Governing Bodies are required to establish disciplinary rules and procedures and for taking steps for making these known to members of staff.

Dismissal

Schedule 16 also provides (in paragraph 25) that where a Governing Body has decided to dismiss an employee, it must notify the local education authority in writing of this decision and the reasons for it.

Paragraph 27 deals in the following terms with the rights of an employee facing dismissal.

"**1)** The Governing Body shall:
    (a) make arrangements for giving any person in respect of whom they propose to make a determination under paragraph 25(1) an opportunity of making representations as to the action they propose to take (including, if he so wishes, oral representations to such person or persons as the Governing Body may appoint for that purpose), and
    (b) have regard to any representations made by him.
2) The Governing Body shall also make arrangements for giving any person in respect of whom they have made a determination under paragraph 25(1) an opportunity of appealing against it before they notify the local education authority of the determination."

Schedule 17 of the Act lays down similar rules in relation to foundation, voluntary aided and foundation special schools. The Governing Bodies of such schools do not have to inform the local education authority of decisions to dismiss employees unless they have accorded advisory rights to the LEA.

The employment relationship in schools

The School Standards and Framework Act 1998 perpetuates the unusual relationship between the staff of locally managed schools and their employers, which has existed since Governing Bodies first took over responsibility for managing staff in the 1980s.

Outside the education sector, the employment relationship is almost always two-sided. On the one side, there is the employee, and on the other, the employer, who is responsible for all aspects of the former's employment. By contrast, in community and voluntary controlled schools, there are three parties to the contract of employment. First, there is the employee. Then, there is the local education authority, which is the contractual employer and has overarching responsibility for conditions of service. However, it is the Governing Body that carries out the employer's day-to-day responsibilities in relation to making appointments, determining disciplinary and grievance procedures and, if necessary, dismissing staff.

This triangular employment relationship is unique to community and voluntary controlled schools. In foundation and aided schools, Governing Bodies are the employers in law as well as in practice, and have a standard two-way contractual relationship with employees. However, they can accord advisory rights to the LEA.

LEA advice

Although the management of employees is the responsibility of the Governing Body of community and voluntary controlled schools, the School Standards and Framework Act 1998 gives local education authorities the right to advise governors whenever disciplinary procedures are used. In foundation schools, the Governing Body can choose to grant the LEA the right to give advice concerning dismissals. The 1998 Act is silent on the question of advisory rights in relation to support and other non-teaching staff. However, where a foundation school is granting the LEA advisory rights in relation to teachers, it would be sensible to extend these rights in relation to non-teaching staff.

Aided schools may also grant the LEA advisory rights. However, if they do, they are automatically obliged to accord similar rights to the relevant diocesan board of education.

Failure to follow an LEA's advice when it has been given can have serious financial implications for a school. If a Governing Body wilfully ignores this advice and then loses an employment tribunal case, the LEA can deduct from the school's budget any sums awarded as compensation. Since the upper limit for compensation in unfair dismissal cases is now £50,000, losing a case can cost a school the equivalent of two teachers' annual salaries, not to mention the damage to the school's good name.

However, schools should not automatically assume that an LEA's advice is always sound. There have been cases where schools have followed their LEA's advice and still lost employment tribunal cases.

Good advice on personnel matters should not be in 'take it or leave it' form. Rather, it should set out the various options and help the school to identify those which accord with the law or good employment practice.

While it is theoretically possible for an individual Governing Body to produce its own set of disciplinary rules and procedures, this is not a wise course of action. As an employer in its own right, the LEA will have a set of procedures, in some cases dating back to the days before local management of schools when it still had responsibility for staff discipline. Assuming these rules and procedures have been updated to take account of the current state of education and employment law, it is a good idea for schools to adopt them. A school with its own procedures is likely to invite questions from trade unions representing employees as to why it is not following established local procedures.

Some LEAs, however, have rather cumbersome and long-winded procedures. Where that is the case, the Governing Body may wish to review the procedures in order to make them more manageable.

The legal background: a summary

- Employees can claim for unfair dismissal after just one year in post.

- Governing Bodies of all maintained schools with delegated budgets have full responsibility for managing and disciplining staff, though legally the LEA is the employer in community and voluntary controlled schools.

- Governing Bodies and senior managers should be aware of the ACAS code of practice, particularly the essential features of disciplinary procedures.

- In community and voluntary controlled schools, the LEA has the right to give advice throughout any disciplinary procedures.

- Foundation and aided schools may give the LEA advisory rights in relation to staff discipline and dismissal.

CHAPTER 4
DISCIPLINARY RULES AND PROCEDURES

Conduct and capability

Some attempts to deal with challenging staff fall at the first hurdle because the school uses misconduct proceedings when the issue is in fact one of capability. It is therefore essential to distinguish between lack of capability and misconduct, though this is sometimes easier said than done. Every manager, and indeed every teacher, will be familiar with situations where it is not clear whether someone cannot or will not act in a certain way. The following examples, all based on situations we have come across in our work with schools, illustrate this dilemma.

Can't or won't?

- The school caretaker has added the wrong chemicals to the swimming pool. As a result, children's hair turns green.

- A science teacher is not marking pupils' work.

- A teacher in the maths department has what appears to be a bottle of whisky in her cupboard and smells strongly of drink.

In all three cases, a careful investigation was needed to establish whether the individual concerned had deliberately acted wrongly or inappropriately.

In the first case, it turned out that the caretaker had not bothered to order the appropriate chemicals for cleaning the school swimming pool and had used what was to hand. This was clearly a case of misconduct and the caretaker received a warning that similar conduct in future could result in his dismissal. A year later, when he again used the wrong chemical, this time in the boys' urinal, he was sacked. However, in another similar case, a caretaker was unable to read the labels on the tins of chemicals, and the LEA was prosecuted for failing to give him appropriate training.

If a teacher has a deliberate policy of not marking pupils' work, that would count as misconduct. However, in our example, it emerged that the science teacher felt snowed under with work and unable to do all his marking. This was a case of capability rather than conduct and the teacher was given the support he needed to improve his performance.

In our third example, the maths teacher who smelled of drink eventually admitted to a history of alcoholism. Her school rightly treated this as a health problem and made sure she sought appropriate professional help. If she had refused help or the investigation had shown that this was not a health issue, it would have been necessary to treat her actions as misconduct.

As these examples show, it can be difficult to distinguish between misconduct and lack of capability. The Employment Appeals Tribunal gave some guidance on this question in 1978 when it held that "employers and tribunals should clearly distinguish in their own minds whether the case in point is one of sheer incapability due to an inherent incapacity to function, or one of failure to exercise to the full such talent as is possessed. Cases where a person has not come up to standard through his own carelessness, negligence or idleness are much more appropriately dealt with as cases of misconduct rather than of incapability."

Under employment law, an employer is obliged to state the principal reason for dismissing an employee. Where there is evidence of misconduct as well as incapability, both should be given as reasons for starting proceedings but the more serious one should be made the principal reason for dismissal.

Ground rules

Disciplinary rules set out the standards of conduct employers expect from employees. They should be written down and reviewed from time to time.

Although the Governing Body is responsible for establishing disciplinary rules and making sure these are known to all the staff of the school, it is good management practice to involve employees and their trade union representatives whenever rules are introduced or reviewed.

Disciplinary rules need to distinguish between the kinds of behaviour that would amount to misconduct on the one hand, and gross misconduct on the other. However, the rules should not attempt to cover every possible type of misconduct and, indeed, most sets of rules will end with a phrase indicating that the list is not exhaustive. This is a recognition that human beings are endlessly inventive and can always come up with forms of behaviour that do not appear on an employer's list! Who, after all, would have imagined a few years ago that anyone would download pornography from the Internet onto a school computer? Yet this has been known to happen.

Gross misconduct and misconduct

Gross misconduct can be defined as behaviour that makes a member of staff's continued employment in a school unacceptable.

Examples of gross misconduct include:
- theft;
- violence towards pupils or colleagues;
- sexual relations with pupils.

Examples of misconduct include:
- persistent lateness;
- unauthorised use of the school's telephone for private calls;
- offensive language directed at colleagues, pupils or other members of the school community.

Other examples of misconduct and gross misconduct are in the model rules included in Appendix A.

Procedures

While disciplinary rules set out standards of conduct, disciplinary procedures are there to ensure that staff keep to these standards. They also provide a fair and consistent method of dealing with misconduct and therefore play a part in promoting good employer-employee relations.

When a teacher is accused of misconduct which is clearly not criminal, the headteacher should carry out an initial investigation to determine whether to take the matter further. The following is designed to guide headteachers through this process.

Investigating allegations of misconduct - a checklist of questions

Q Has a deputy head or other senior member of staff been delegated to carry out the investigation?

A If so, the governors should not rely solely on that person's report in any disciplinary hearing. Witnesses to the alleged misconduct or direct evidence should be produced.

Q Does the investigation show that the allegations are unfounded?

A If so, the matter can be quietly dropped.

Q Does the investigation reveal a prima facie cause for complaint?

A If it does, the headteacher should inform the employee of the complaint and the possibility that it could lead to disciplinary action. The head should then ask for the employee's side of the story.

Q Is the alleged misconduct serious?

A If it is, the employee should be offered the opportunity to be accompanied when meeting the headteacher to discuss the allegations.

Q Is the employee obliged to say anything at this meeting?

A No, but he or she should be told that, while silence does not denote guilt, it is likely to leave the head with no alternative but to start disciplinary proceedings.

Q What if the employee admits having behaved wrongly or inappropriately?

A In that case, there will usually be no need for further investigation. The employee should be asked to confirm the admission in writing. If he or she refuses, a full investigation should be carried out.

Q Can an employee be forced to resign?

A No. If an employee admits to gross misconduct or to misconduct after a final warning, it may be appropriate to give him or her an opportunity to resign. However, pressurising an employee to resign could result in a successful claim for 'constructive dismissal', a fundamental breach of the employment contract by the employer. Saying to an employee, "resign or be sacked", counts as dismissal in law.

Q Should evidence of misconduct always lead to disciplinary proceedings?

A No. Even when there is evidence to support the allegations or an employee admits to misconduct, the head will still need to assess its seriousness and consider any mitigating circumstances before deciding whether to take the matter further.

Criminal offences at work

If, at any stage of an internal investigation, the headteacher has sufficient reason to believe that an employee may have committed a criminal offence, the police should be informed straight away. The employee should then be suspended on normal pay.

The criminal legal process operates quite independently of any parallel disciplinary process in the workplace, so it is not necessarily unfair to dismiss an employee for gross misconduct if he or she is still awaiting trial for the same offence. Neither is dismissal following conviction for a criminal offence at work automatically deemed fair in employment law. Should the employee decide to challenge the employer's decision, it will be judged on its merits by an employment tribunal, not by a criminal court. In other words, criminal proceedings are no excuse for short-circuiting normal disciplinary procedures.

Criminal offences outside work

Conviction for a criminal offence outside work should not be treated as an automatic reason for dismissal. The headteacher should consider whether the nature of the offence makes the individual concerned unfit for his or her job or unacceptable to other employees.

Employees should not be dismissed solely because a charge against them is pending or because they have been remanded in custody and so cannot attend work.

Suspending teachers suspected of gross misconduct

If an initial investigation shows that, on the balance of probability, a member of staff has behaved in a way that amounts to gross misconduct, he or she should be suspended on full pay.

Any delay in suspending an employee suspected of gross misconduct is likely to compromise the governors' position at a subsequent dismissal hearing. It would allow the employee to argue that, if the alleged misdemeanour really had amounted to gross misconduct, the governors would not have allowed him or her to carry on working at the school.

The following case study illustrates how difficult it is to dismiss employees for gross misconduct if they have not been suspended as soon as their misdemeanour became known.

A helping hand

A modern languages teacher gave his pupils a preview of some of the trickier words in a GCSE aural examination that they were due to take a few days later. The school's headteacher discovered what had happened and, having taken advice, took the view that this was a case of gross misconduct. He did not, however, suspend the teacher immediately as he needed him to continue to teach until after that year's A-level examinations.

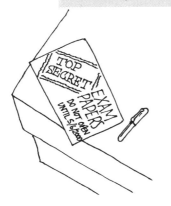

This turned out to be fatal to the case for dismissing the teacher. At a governors' dismissal hearing, the teacher argued that, by allowing him to continue doing his job, the head had tacitly admitted that the misdemeanour was not all that serious, and did not warrant dismissal.

The headteacher of a community or voluntary controlled school should seek advice from the LEA before suspending a member of staff. The LEA should also be informed of a decision to suspend. This also applies to foundation and aided schools which have given LEAs advisory rights.

The head should provide a written confirmation of the decision to suspend immediately after conveying it verbally to the employee. This letter should inform the employee of the suspension, specify the nature of the complaint and explain that it could lead to dismissal without notice.

Model letter confirming a suspension

Dear Mr Green,

I am writing to confirm that, after receiving complaints that you have been falsifying your timesheets, you are suspended from your employment as caretaker of this school as of today, 24 June 2000. You will remain suspended on full pay pending further investigation into these complaints and, if necessary, a disciplinary hearing before the staff dismissal committee of the school's Governing Body. The suspension is a neutral act and does not imply that you are guilty of the allegations.

The allegations against you are that on two occasions last term (27 January 2000 and 12 March 2000) and on one occasion this term (24 May), you were seen in the King's Head public house at times when, according to the timesheets you later completed, you were engaged in maintenance work on the school premises.

If my investigation reveals grounds for holding a disciplinary hearing, you will be given 10 days' notice of the date and time of this hearing.

If the dismissal committee of the Governing Body finds that the complaint against you is justified, you may be dismissed without notice for gross misconduct, unless there are mitigating circumstances.

Only the Governing Body and the headteacher have the power to suspend a member of staff. However, the full governing body should not be involved in the decision to suspend as this would prejudice any subsequent move to discipline or dismiss the individual concerned or hear an appeal against dismissal. In practice, therefore, it is likely to be the headteacher, the chair of governors or another governor, such as the vice chair or the chair of a committee, who would suspend a member of staff. It would, in any event, be sensible for the headteacher to discuss a possible suspension with the chair of governors in the first instance.

Neither the headteacher nor the LEA has the power to lift a suspension. Again, this rests with the Governing Body. The LEA must be informed when a member of staff in a community or voluntary controlled school is suspended and may give the Governing Body advice, but it has no other role to play in a suspension.

Once the decision to lift a suspension has been taken, the employee should be informed of this in writing and will normally be asked to return to work straight away. The employee should also be informed that the letter of suspension and any other written material relating to the allegations will be destroyed. Headteachers should make sure that no copy of this final communication is placed in the employee's personal file. Data protection legislation now gives employees the right to see their personnel records, and an employee may have a legitimate grievance if material relating to such a matter is kept on file.

Suspension is intended to enable an employer to conduct an unfettered investigation into allegations against an employee, and is regarded in law as a neutral act. However, when 'mud' starts flying around a staff room, some of it is likely to stick. The decision to suspend must therefore be carefully judged in relation to the facts available at the time.

No smoke without fire?

The headteacher of a small primary school overheard two 10 year-old girls apparently alleging that a male teacher had had some sort of sexual contact with another child. The girls did not name the teacher, but the head consulted the chair of governors, who immediately suspended the school's only male teacher.

On questioning the two girls, the head discovered that they had in fact been discussing a particularly torrid episode of a popular television soap opera. The teacher was reinstated straight away, but rumours about his conduct persisted and strains began to appear in his marriage.

A previously successful and enthusiastic member of staff, he was eventually diagnosed with clinical depression and took early retirement on grounds of ill-health.

Suspension and child protection

In recent years, a greater awareness of child protection issues has led to a steep rise in the number of teachers and other school employees accused of physically or sexually abusing children. Such accusations should not automatically lead to suspension. However, suspension will be appropriate where:

- the allegations are serious enough to constitute gross misconduct;
- it is necessary for an investigation into the allegations to proceed unimpeded;
- children could be at risk.

When considering suspension, the headteacher should advise the member of staff concerned to seek assistance from his or her union. The head should also consult the school's personnel advisor before entering this legal and emotional minefield.

The whole issue of child protection is the subject of another handbook in the Education Personnel Management series.

Dismissal for gross misconduct

Although gross misconduct is conduct so serious that it justifies dismissal without previous warning and without any notice, no employee can be dismissed without a hearing and in schools that must be before a committee of governors. The conduct of disciplinary hearings is considered in the next chapter.

Disciplinary procedures - the informal stage

Most disciplinary procedures include an 'informal stage' which is outside the formal disciplinary procedure. Variously referred to as a 'verbal' or an 'oral' warning, this is intended to serve as a managerial warning shot and should not be too friendly or casual in tone. The employee must be left in no doubt that he or she has been warned, so it is sensible to send a memorandum of the meeting at which the warning was made. An example follows.

A shot across the bows

Memorandum

To: Tony West, head of
           science
From: James Waltham,
           headteacher
Date: 3 June 2000

Further to our meeting yesterday, I am writing to confirm the points I made about your conduct in the staffroom last Friday.

Staff at this school are expected to set an example to pupils. It is unacceptable for any member of staff to address a colleague in the way that you addressed Sandra Harris during last week's science department meeting. I was particularly concerned that pupils might have heard the abusive language you used.

Please note that I warned you verbally that any repetition of such behaviour will lead to formal disciplinary proceedings against you.

Some procedures offer a right of appeal against a verbal warning but this is perhaps in conflict with the idea of firing a warning shot across the employee's bows.

Whatever procedure a school adopts, it should be applied consistently. Any action taken by a headteacher sets a precedent by which future decisions will be measured. So, if one employee's misdemeanour is dealt with informally, others who behave in a similar way should receive the same treatment.

Most minor cases of staff misconduct can be resolved informally. However, to avoid neglecting other aspects of their work, school managers need to set some limits on the amount of time and effort they invest in people who have overstepped the mark. These individuals can be as draining of time and energy as disruptive pupils, and there comes a time when informal guidance has to give way to formal disciplinary procedures.

Disciplinary procedures - the formal stages

Normally, a first written warning is the first formal disciplinary penalty. Local procedures vary, and in some cases the headteacher is empowered only to give a verbal warning, while the written warning has to come from the Governing Body. This type of procedure undermines the head's managerial role and places a heavy burden on governors, since it means they have to convene a committee to consider every stage in the disciplinary procedure beyond the initial verbal warning.

Where Governing Bodies do issue written warnings themselves, they need to make sure they are left with enough members to sit on separate committees to issue warnings, to consider dismissal and to hear appeals against warnings and dismissals. This can present a particular difficulty for primary schools with relatively small Governing Bodies.

The next stage in most misconduct procedures is a final written warning. Again, procedures vary, with some giving the headteacher the power to issue this warning and others giving it to the Governing Body alone.

ACAS advises that warnings should normally expire after one year. However, where child protection issues are involved, allowing a warning to expire so quickly can be inappropriate. Governing Bodies would therefore be well advised to include in their disciplinary procedures a statement to the effect that, where children's safety or well-being is at stake, warnings will remain in force for longer periods and, in exceptional cases, indefinitely.

Where the series of warnings fails to produce an improvement in the employee's conduct, a school's Governing Body is entitled to move on to the next stage, a dismissal hearing before a panel of at least three governors.

The employee has the right to appeal against a dismissal decision. This appeal, the final stage in the procedure, would need to be heard by a panel of governors who had not previously been involved in the case. The appeals panel must be made up of at least as many governors as the panel which first considered dismissal.

Dealing with misconduct: the five stages

1. Recorded verbal warning, with a right of appeal if provided for under the school's procedures.

2. First written warning (from the headteacher or governors), with right of appeal to the appeals committee of the Governing Body.

3. Final written warning (from the headteacher or governors), with right of appeal to the governors' appeals committee.

4. Dismissal by the governors' dismissal committee.

5. Appeal against dismissal to the governors' appeals committee.

The employee's rights

At each stage of the disciplinary process, the employee is entitled to know precisely what it is that he or she has been accused of doing. The employee also has the right to have the matter properly investigated. This investigation should be carried out by someone who is not involved in making decisions at any stage of the disciplinary process. So, if the headteacher has the power to issue warnings up to the level of the final written warning, the investigation is best carried out by the deputy head or another senior member of staff.

The employee has a right to put his or her side of the case in person and to bring a 'friend' to hearings held during the formal stages of the procedures. Local procedures will specify whether there are any constraints on who that person might be. Sometimes the 'friend' has to be a representative of their trade union or a work colleague. Occasionally, local procedures will specify whether or not a solicitor or a relative is allowed to accompany the employee to a formal hearing. Employees also have the right to call witnesses on their own behalf.

Summary of the employee's rights

An employee accused of misconduct or gross misconduct has the right to:

- know the full accusation;
- have the matter properly investigated;
- be heard;
- be accompanied or represented at any hearing;
- call witnesses;
- appeal to the Governing Body's appeals committee against dismissal or a written warning.

As a society, we are becoming increasingly litigious, and teachers are not immune to this trend. School managers should therefore be aware that if they fail to go through all the stages of the disciplinary procedure recommended by ACAS, they may have to justify their actions to an employment tribunal.

CHAPTER 5
DISCIPLINARY
HEARINGS

Procedural errors in the process leading up to dismissal are the most common reason for employment tribunals finding in favour of employees in unfair dismissal cases. For a school to lose an employment tribunal case can be a public relations disaster that damages both teacher and pupil recruitment. It is therefore essential to 'dot every i and cross every t' throughout the series of hearings and appeals that need to be held when a school employee is accused of misconduct or gross misconduct. Any temptation to cut procedural corners in order to reach a quick resolution should be resisted.

A cautionary tale

A few years ago, the newly-appointed headteacher of what was then a grant-maintained school introduced management changes that proved unpopular with some of her senior staff. Eventually, after accusing the head of a number of management failings, the governors decided to take the day-to-day running of the school away from her and give it to a group of senior staff.

The headteacher tried to continue working in accordance with her statutory terms and conditions of employment, which give heads responsibility for the day-to-day management of their schools. Consequently, she was suspended and asked to attend a dismissal hearing before a panel of governors.

The chair of governors set up the dismissal panel without first convening a full meeting of the Governing Body. This was a breach of education law, which clearly states that responsibility for dismissing staff (and for hearing appeals against dismissal) resides with the Governing Body, which must delegate this responsibility to a specially constituted panel. By acting unilaterally, the chair of governors was, in effect, preventing the Governing Body from discharging its responsibility.

On discovering that the dismissal panel had not been properly constituted, the headteacher's union applied to the High Court for an injunction to stop the panel from holding the hearing. This was granted, with the court instructing the Governing Body to convene a new panel in accordance with the law. However, the school's chair of governors again appointed her own panel, which decided to sack the headteacher. The head's union promptly went back to the High Court for a second injunction to stop the Governing Body from acting on this decision. The union also asked that the chair of governors and another governor be jailed for contempt of court.

Although these two governors were spared a sojourn in prison, the court ordered the Governing Body to pay the union's substantial legal costs. The headteacher remained suspended until her union succeeded in negotiating an unusually large financial settlement on her behalf. Procedural errors cost this school dear.

Who does what?

Governors

Governing Bodies are strongly advised to delegate the management of disciplinary matters up to and including the level of final written warning to the headteacher. To do otherwise would undermine the head's ability to manage staff and could leave the Governing Body prejudiced when hearing a case for dismissal.

The Governing Body should set up a panel consisting of at least three governors. Described as the 'staff dismissal committee' in the School Governors' Regulations 1999, this panel will have the following responsibilities:

- to consider those staff disciplinary matters not delegated to the headteacher, including any proposal to dismiss an employee;

- to consider cases referred by the headteacher or cases that the panel itself may decide to consider;

- to lift a suspension, if the decision is not to dismiss.

The Governing Body should also set up a panel to consider appeals against dismissal or any other formal disciplinary action against an employee. The appeals panel should consist of at least the same number of governors as the staff dismissal committee or, if the appeal is against a decision made by the headteacher, at least three governors. Since natural justice demands that no governor involved in making the original decision should hear an appeal against it, the two panels should be made up of different people.

The appeals committee should hear an appeal before any action is taken to implement the dismissal committee's decision to dismiss a member of staff. The committee's decisions should always be minuted.

Where the headteacher's own conduct is the subject of a complaint, the chair of governors will need to act as the head's line manager, and should not sit on the panel considering the alleged misconduct.

The headteacher

Where the Governing Body has delegated the management of disciplinary matters up to and including the level of final written warning, the headteacher has the following duties and powers:

- to initiate disciplinary action short of dismissal;

- to arrange and conduct disciplinary hearings;

- to suspend, on full pay, any person employed to work at the school who is suspected of gross misconduct;

- to inform the Governing Body immediately of any suspension. In community and voluntary controlled schools, the LEA should also be informed.

The LEA

The LEA has a duty to give the Governing Bodies of community and voluntary controlled schools advice in respect of dismissal proceedings.

Arranging a disciplinary hearing

Disciplinary hearings should be held as soon as possible after a complaint has been made about an employee. It is good practice to consult the employee and his or her representative on the date for a hearing or an appeal.

An example of a letter summoning an employee to a disciplinary hearing is included in the case study at the end of this chapter. The headteacher's letter summoning the employee to a hearing has to comply with the requirements laid down in the school's disciplinary procedure. So if, for example, a school using the model procedure in Appendix B sends out a letter and fails to provide the employee with copies of documents due to be used in evidence, the employee may ask for the hearing to be postponed until this evidence has been produced.

Similarly, the headteacher should also ask for advance notice of any documentary evidence the employee intends to use at the hearing, together with the names of any witnesses who may be called. The head may postpone the hearing until this information has been supplied.

A disciplinary hearing conducted by the headteacher

The headteacher should normally conduct the hearing, preferably accompanied by a personnel specialist or other individual qualified to advise on procedure and on the merits of the case. This professional adviser, who may be employed by the LEA or another organisation contracted to provide personnel services to the school, may put questions to witnesses during the hearing, if authorised to do so by the headteacher. Where the Governing Body has delegated responsibility for managing staff discipline to the headteacher, the final decision on the result of the hearing rests with the headteacher alone.

The headteacher should begin by clearly setting out the reasons for holding the hearing and explaining how it will be conducted.

The facts supporting the complaint should then be presented, together with any written documents that are available. Witnesses who can support the headteacher's allegations or those made by someone else should also be called at this stage. The employee or his or her representative should then be allowed to question each witness in turn, including the headteacher if appropriate. Witnesses other than the headteacher must withdraw after giving their evidence.

Once all of the evidence against the employee has been presented, the employee or their representative must be given the opportunity to present his or her case, together with evidence to support it. The employee will normally give evidence but is under no compulsion to do so. If the employee has given evidence, the headteacher will need to question him or her directly. Again, witnesses other than the employee should withdraw once they have had their say.

After giving their evidence, the employee or the employee's representative should be allowed to sum up the reasons why the complaint should not be found justified.

The headteacher may decide to adjourn the hearing at any stage to enable either side to carry our further investigations. This adjournment may be at the employee's request.

The employee and the employee's representative should withdraw while the headteacher, preferably with the adviser present, decides what to do. It is sometimes necessary to recall witness from either side to clear up points of uncertainty. If this happens, the employee and the representative must be recalled at the same time and may question recalled witnesses.

The headteacher's decision should be based on the facts presented at the hearing, and take account of any mitigating circumstances, such as provocation, domestic and health factors. The employee's previous record and length of service also needs to be taken into account. A person with a previously unblemished record who is going through a crisis at home should obviously be treated more leniently than someone whose attitude or conduct have long been a cause for concern.

In making a decision, the headteacher has the following options:

1. to find the complaint not justified;

2. to find the complaint justified and
   a) to issue no warning at all (perhaps because of strong mitigating circumstances or the unlikelihood of similar misconduct occurring in the future);
   b) to issue an oral warning;
   c) to issue a formal, written warning, subject to the provisions of the school's disciplinary procedure;
   d) to decide that the employee's conduct appears to amount to gross misconduct, to suspend the individual and refer the matter to the Governing Body as soon as possible.

The burden of proof

Some school governors and headteachers mistakenly assume that they can only uphold a complaint against an employee if, as in a criminal case, guilt has been proved beyond all reasonable doubt. In fact, employment tribunals have established that employers need only show that their decisions are reasonable in all the circumstances of a given misconduct case. So if, for example, a teacher accused of driving the school van while under the influence of alcohol had been seen drinking out of a large green bottle, the contents of which looked and smelled like gin, there would be no need to send it to a forensic laboratory for analysis before taking disciplinary action.

Getting to the truth

So far in this chapter, we have concentrated on procedural matters. Conducting a disciplinary hearing, however, is not simply a question of following the right procedures. Since the aim of a disciplinary hearing is to establish the truth, it is also important to create an atmosphere in which all the relevant facts will emerge. So, while the tone of the hearing will inevitably be formal, the employee should also be encouraged to talk freely.

Open questions usually achieve this objective more readily than closed questions, which should be used sparingly and only when very specific information is required. For example, a question such as, "What did you do with the dinner money after you had collected it?" will probably elicit more information than the question, "Did the dinner money go straight into your pocket?"

Disciplinary hearings do not always go smoothly. With their jobs on the line, some employees become distressed or angry. When this happens, they should be given time to compose themselves. If necessary, the hearing should be adjourned until a later date. However, in extreme circumstances, an employee's aggressive behaviour during a hearing may itself become the subject of further disciplinary action.

Those conducting the hearing should never allow themselves to be drawn into arguments or to behave in ways that might be construed as bullying.

Moonlighting

Mike Stewart was employed as a class teacher and music co-ordinator at West Newtown Junior School.

At the beginning of the autumn term, he sent in a medical certificate with a letter explaining that during the summer holiday he had hurt his right arm and shoulder in an accident, and would be unable to return to work. The school arranged for a supply teacher to cover his classes and Mike continued to send in medical certificates.

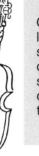

On 16 January, while attending a concert at the local leisure centre, Jemma Owen, another teacher at the school, noticed that the orchestra's cellist was none other than Mike Stewart. The following week, the school's deputy head, Simon How, rang Mike to discuss the matter, but discovered from his flatmate that Mike was "on a canoeing holiday".

After some investigation, Mike received the following letter.

Dear Mr Stewart,
Disciplinary hearing
Your attendance is required at a hearing before the dismissal committee of the Governing Body to be held on Monday, 20 February 2000 at 10 a.m. in the school.

The purpose of the hearing is to consider a complaint of gross misconduct against you, in that, while you were away from work on certified sickness absence, you:

(1)   played a musical instrument at a public concert, an activity which is inconsistent with the reason for absence stated on your medical certificates, and
(2)   you were on a canoeing holiday.

You have the right to be accompanied or represented at the hearing by a representative of your trade union or any other person of your choice.

The following documents will be produced at the hearing:
- medical certificates;
- witness statements from Miss Jemma Owen and Mr Simon How, deputy headteacher.

In addition, the following witnesses will be called:
- Mrs Elaine Southam, headteacher;
- Mr Edward Brook, conductor, Eastern Chamber Orchestra.

The case for the school will be presented by Mrs Margaret Johnson, the school's personnel consultant. Mr Peter Norton, of the County Council's education department, will also be present to advise the committee of governors.

Would you please let me know as soon as possible whether or not you will be represented and, if so, the name and position of your representative.

You have the right to produce documentary evidence and to call witnesses on your own behalf. Please forward to me, at least 14 days before the hearing, the names of any witnesses you intend to call, together with copies of documents you intend to produce. A copy of the procedure to be followed at the hearing is attached.

You should be aware that the dismissal committee of the Governing Body has the power to dismiss you from your post if it finds the complaint against you justified. If you do not attend the hearing without good cause, the panel may decide to proceed in your absence.

Yours sincerely,

E.J. Smith, Clerk to the governors.

During the hearing, the following two witness statements were produced.

Statement by Miss Jemma Owen

On Saturday 16 January 2000, I attended a concert in the Newtown Leisure Centre with my fiance. We had seats near the front of the stalls, from where members of the orchestra were clearly visible. Soon after the concert started, I noticed the cellist, whom I recognised as my colleague, Mike Stewart.

At the end of concert, we went to the bar adjoining the concert hall. After we had been there for a few minutes, some of the musicians entered, among them Mike. I said "Hello, Mike", and he nodded in reply. I then said I would see him soon.

Statement by Mr Simon How

On Tuesday 19 January 2000, I was asked by the headteacher, Mrs Southam, to telephone Mike Stewart to see if he knew when he would be returning to work, as the supply teacher we were employing to cover his lessons would be leaving and we needed to make other arrangements.

When I rang Mike, the telephone was answered by his flatmate, Richard Fawcett, who expressed surprise at my call. He said that Mike was on a canoeing trip.

I passed this information on to Mrs Southam.

At the disciplinary hearing, Mike admitted that he had gone away for a long weekend's canoeing and had played a musical instrument at a public concert while on sick leave. He argued through his union representative that these activities formed part of his rehabilitation and recovery from the serious injuries he had sustained in the accident. No medical evidence was presented.

After the hearing, he received the following letter from the adviser to the governors' dismissal committee.

21 February 2000

Dear Mr Stewart,

Dismissal letter

I am writing to confirm the decision of the committee of governors at the dismissal hearing on Monday 20 February 2000 at which you were represented by Mr O'Brien.

The panel took the most serious view of your conduct in undertaking a professional musical performance and going canoeing while on certified sickness absence from your employment as a teacher. The panel unanimously agreed that this showed a most serious lack of commitment that they would not have expected from a professional teacher, and that it amounted to gross misconduct.

The panel considered the mitigating circumstances put to them on your behalf by your representative, but decided to dismiss you from your post summarily.

You have the right to appeal against this decision to the appeals panel of the Governing Body. If you decide to exercise this right, you should inform the clerk to the governors within 10 working days.

Yours sincerely,

Margaret Johnson, Personnel Consultant

CHAPTER 6
THE ROLE OF GOVERNORS

Managing staff

The day-to-day running of a school, including the management of staff, should be left to its headteacher. However, education law gives the Governing Bodies of all maintained schools ultimate responsibility for managing teaching and non-teaching staff who are paid out of the school budget.

We strongly advise every Governing Body to set up a committee to carry out its responsibilities for personnel matters, even though there is no legal obligation to do so.

In relation to staff discipline, the personnel committee's role is to make sure that suitable disciplinary rules and procedures are adopted and that these are reviewed from time to time. It is good practice to consult staff whenever new rules and procedures are introduced or existing ones amended.

Staff discipline

Disciplinary matters up to and including the level of final written warning are best left to the school's headteacher. However, if the headteacher's own conduct is called into question, the chair of governors will need to act as the head's line manager and issue a verbal warning and, if necessary, a first written warning. When all else fails, the case must be referred to the Governing Body's dismissal committee.

If the complaint against the headteacher is so serious that it may amount to gross misconduct justifying summary dismissal, the chair of governors must suspend the head pending further investigation and, if necessary, a hearing before the dismissal committee.

Dismissal

By law, the Governing Body must set up a staff dismissal committee with delegated power to dismiss members of staff whose conduct is found to be unacceptable. The Governing Body is also obliged to set up a separate appeals committee with delegated powers to hear any appeals against dismissals and final written warnings.

The work of these two committees is often highly technical, so Governing Bodies should make sure that they have access to good quality advice about staff dismissal and, indeed, personnel issues generally. Local education authorities are able to provide personnel services but there may be a case for 'shopping around' for the best available advice, which may come from private sector providers. Training also has an important role to play in ensuring that members of the governors' dismissal and appeals committees have a sound understanding of the role they might be required to play.

Discipline and dismissal - a checklist for governors

	Yes/No	Action Required
Has the Governing Body adopted and minuted disciplinary rules and procedures?		
Have these rules and procedures been reviewed recently?		
Has the Governing Body set up a staff dismissal committee?		
Has the Governing Body set up a separate appeals committee?		
Do the members of the dismissal and appeals committees have a good grasp of their role?		

APPENDIX A
MODEL DISCIPLINARY
RULES FOR ALL EMPLOYEES

(For all employees, whether teaching or not, contracted to work at the school under the School Standards and Framework Act 1998)

1. Gross Misconduct

Gross misconduct is the committing of an act which renders it inadvisable for the employee to be allowed to remain at work. Any employee suspected of committing an act of gross misconduct, as indicated in the list below, will be suspended with full pay pending investigation. If, after proper investigation, it is decided that the employee has committed an act of gross misconduct or if the employee admits the act, s/he will be dismissed without further warning, unless there are mitigating circumstances. The disciplinary procedure must be followed in all cases.

The list of examples below is not intended to be exclusive or exhaustive and offences of a similar gravity will receive the same treatment.

1.1 Dishonesty associated with place of work or job being undertaken:

(a) theft of property belonging to the School, the Local Education Authority, a Contractor, an employee or a pupil;

(b) deliberate falsification of timesheets or expenses claims for pecuniary advantage;

(c) demanding or accepting monies or other considerations as a bribe for the use of School or Local Education Authority property, provision of School or Local Education Authority service or the showing of favour on behalf of the School or Local Education Authority;

(d) falsification of any information given on an application form for a post to gain advantage whether pecuniary or otherwise;

(e) failure to disclose criminal convictions not exempt under the terms of the Rehabilitation of Offenders Act, 1975;

(f) falsification of registration of pupils or students for pecuniary gain.

1.2 Deliberate refusal to carry out a reasonable, lawful and safe instruction or the normal agreed defined duties of the post.

1.3 Gross negligence in failing to attend to or carry out the agreed duties of the post.

1.4 Wilfully ignoring responsibilities/instructions, thus placing other employees/pupils in danger, e.g. ignoring handling instructions/safety regulations in respect of radioactive materials.

1.5 Being unfit to perform duties associated with the post as a result of taking drugs, other than in accordance with medical advice, or taking alcohol.

1.6 Wilful unauthorised disclosure of information (classified as confidential), by employees who, in the course of their duties, have access to such information which, by its release, could be harmful to the School, Local Education Authority, other employees or pupils.

1.7 Acts of violence or vandalism in the course of employment:

(a) malicious damage to School/ Local Education Authority/ Contractors'/ other employees'/ pupils' property;

(b) actual physical violence towards members/officers of the Authority, members of the school staff/governors/parents/pupils/other members of the public;

1.8 Sexual misconduct at work:

(a) sexual misconduct, whether criminal or not;

(b) sexual relations with students.

1.9 Off-duty misconduct:

(a) an act of criminal sexual misconduct by an employee who, in the course of duty, has contact with young people;

(b) drug offences committed by employees whose job brings them into contact with young people;

(c) sexual relations with students, or young persons.

2. Misconduct

Misconduct is of a degree less serious than that which would warrant immediate suspension from duty for a first offence but which could nevertheless lead to dismissal if persistent. The disciplinary procedure must be followed when dealing with misconduct. Some more serious acts of misconduct might justify omitting the first stage of disciplinary procedures by issuing a final warning in the first instance, if there is no satisfactory explanation. Only when it can be shown that the warnings have not been heeded will misconduct lead to action being taken which will lead to an employee's dismissal.

The list of examples below is not intended to be exclusive or exhaustive and offences of a similar gravity will receive the same treatment.

2.1 Absenteeism and lateness, for example:

(a) failure to remain at the place of work during normal working hours without permission or sufficient cause for absence;

(b) frequent failure to attend work punctually;

(c) failure to notify the school immediately or as soon as reasonably practicable when absence is due to sickness;

(d) failure to provide medical certificates in accordance with the Conditions of Service.

2.2 Dishonesty and petty wrongs, for example:

(a) making unauthorised private telephone calls and/or sending personal mail at the establishment's expense;

(b) failure to report any loss and/or damage to any property issued to or by the employee in connection with his/her employment.

2.3 Neglect of duty, for example:

    (a) failure to adopt safe working practices/use protective equipment where required by law or management;

    (b) negligent use of school property in such a way as is likely to cause serious damage or loss;

    (c) failure to discharge without sufficient cause the obligations which statute or the contract of employment places on the employee;

    (d) insubordination;

    (e) failure to exercise proper control or supervision of pupils or students.

2.4 Abusive behaviour/offensive language which arises directly out of or in connection with work and which is directed at members/officers of the Authority, colleagues, governors, pupils or members of the public.

2.5 Victimisation of other employees in the course of duty.

2.6 Unlawful discrimination against other employees, pupils or members of the public in the course of duty.

2.7 Discrimination, whether unlawful or not, in the course of duty against other employees, pupils or members of the public on the grounds of sex, marital status, ethnic origin, disability or sexual orientation.

2.8 Undertaking additional employment outside normal working hours which would be detrimental to the work to be performed as a full time employee of the Local Education Authority.

APPENDIX B
MODEL DISCIPLINARY PROCEDURE RELATING TO MISCONDUCT

(For all employees other than the headteacher)

To be read in conjunction with the School Government Regulations 1999

1. Definitions

1.1 The term 'headteacher' also refers to any other title used to identify the headteacher where appropriate.

1.2 The term 'employee' refers to any member of the staff, whether teaching or not (with the exception of the headteacher or acting headteacher), employed to work at the school.

1.3 'Misconduct' is defined in the Disciplinary Rules which accompany the Misconduct Procedure.

2. Oral Warning

2.1 Misconduct is defined in the Disciplinary Rules, to which reference should be made. The following procedure does not relate to oral warnings which might be given to the employee by the headteacher. However, repeated misconduct after an oral warning would normally lead to more serious disciplinary action in accordance with the procedure. There is no appeal against an oral warning.

3. First Written Warning

3.1 Where the headteacher considers on the preliminary facts that formal disciplinary action for misconduct, but not gross misconduct, is necessary, s/he will write to the employee to inform him/her, at least 10 working days in advance, setting out:

(a) the date, time and place of the disciplinary hearing;

(b) the nature of the complaint;

(c) the employee's right to be accompanied by his/her representative of an independent trade union or some other person of his/her choice;

(d) the titles of enclosed copies of any documents to be used as evidence;

(e) the names of any witnesses to be called by the headteacher;

(f) his/her right to call witnesses on his/her behalf.

At the employee's request, an extra copy of this notice, together with any enclosures, should be provided for his/her representative.

3.2 At the disciplinary hearing, the employee (and his/her representative) will be given a reasonable opportunity to state his/her case and to question the headteacher and any witnesses. At the conclusion, the headteacher will state his/her decision and his/her reasons and will soon afterwards confirm them in writing to the employee and his/her representative.

3.3 If s/he decides the complaint was justified, the headteacher may give the employee a first written warning which will include a statement that any further complaint of misconduct occurring within the next twelve months and found justified after a disciplinary hearing will lead to a final warning, unless there are mitigating circumstances.

3.4 If the employee is given no further written warning of misconduct within twelve months of the date of the first written warning, then this warning is disregarded and the warning letter will make this clear.

4. Final Written Warning
4.1 If a further complaint is made about the employee's conduct within twelve months of the date of the first written warning, the same procedure (as at 3.1 and 3.2 above) will be followed.

4.2 If the headteacher decides at the conclusion of the disciplinary hearing that this further complaint is justified, s/he may give the employee a final written warning, which will include a statement that any further complaint of misconduct occurring within the next twelve months and found justified after a disciplinary hearing will lead to dismissal, unless there are mitigating circumstances.

4.3 Again, this final warning, together with any previous warning, will be disregarded if there is no further complaint about misconduct within twelve months of the date of the final warning, and the warning letter will make this clear.

5. Dismissal
5.1 If the headteacher receives or makes a further complaint within twelve months from the date of the final warning, the complaint will be referred to a hearing before the dismissal committee which must consist of at least three Governors, following the procedure in paragraphs 3.1 and 3.2 (above). (For community schools or where advisory rights have been accorded by a foundation or aided school, the Panel will consider any advice given by the LEA.)

5.2 If the dismissal committee decides the complaint is justified, it may decide to dismiss the employee. The dismissal committee will state its decision and its reasons and will soon afterwards confirm them in writing to the employee (and his/her representative).

5.3 If the decision is to dismiss, the employee must be given an opportunity to appeal (see paragraph 7.3). If no appeal is made, or the appeal is unsuccessful, the governors then notify the LEA in writing that s/he is to be dismissed, whether with or without notice, or with pay in lieu of notice. The LEA must give written notice to the employee within 14 days of notification by the Governors.

6. Gross Misconduct
6.1 If the complaint is considered so serious that it may amount to gross misconduct, justifying dismissal without previous warning and without notice (see the Disciplinary Rules), the employee will be informed by the headteacher that s/he is suspended on full pay pending further investigation of the complaint before the dismissal committee who, if they consider the complaint constitutes gross misconduct, will decide to dismiss the employee. The procedure to be followed will be as in previous paragraphs (5.1 to 5.3).

7. Right of Appeal

7.1 The employee has a right of appeal against a written warning issued by the headteacher (see paragraphs 3.3 and 4.2), but not by the governors (see paragraph 8.5). The appeal will be heard by the appeal committee of the governors. They can either confirm the warning or cancel it.

7.2 The employee has a right of appeal against a decision to dismiss issued by the dismissal committee of the governors (see paragraph 5.2). The appeal is to the appeal committee of the governors referred to in 7.1 (above).

7.3 The employee's notice of appeal, stating the grounds for the appeal, should be sent to the clerk to the governors within 10 working days of the receipt of the written decision.

7.4 Appeal hearings will be held as soon as possible after receipt of the appeal.

8. Variation in Penalties

8.1 The headteacher or the appeal committee of the governors may decide to give an oral warning instead of a written warning.

8.2 The headteacher may decide that the first misconduct is so serious that it justifies a first and final written warning.

8.3 The headteacher may decide to issue a further final warning rather than refer the complaint to the dismissal committee of the governors.

8.4 The dismissal committee may decide to issue a further final warning rather than dismiss.

8.5 The appeal committee of the governors may decide to issue a further final warning rather than dismiss, and that such a warning may last for a specified period longer than the original twelve months of the previous final warning, if appropriate. There is no right of appeal against a decision of the appeal committee of the governors.

8.6 In cases of alleged gross misconduct, the dismissal committee or appeal committee may decide to issue a final warning rather than to dismiss.

9. Trade Union Officials

9.1 Although normal disciplinary standards must apply to the conduct of a trade union official as an employee, no disciplinary action beyond an oral warning should be taken until the circumstances of the case have been discussed with the relevant full-time trade union officer.

10. Confidentiality

10.1 The proceedings of this disciplinary procedure shall remain confidential to the parties concerned. Only the decision of a disciplinary hearing or appeal may be reported.

APPENDIX C
USEFUL ADDRESSES

Advisory Conciliation and Arbitration Service
ACAS Head Office
Brandon House
180 Borough High Street
London SE1 1LW
Telephone 020 7396 5100
(Customer Enquiry Line for London region)
For most enquiries, contact your own regional office
(under Dept of Trade and Industry)

Education Personnel Management
St John's House
Spitfire Close
Ermine Business Park
Huntingdon
Cambridgeshire PE18 6EP
Telephone 01480 431993
Fax 01480 431992
E-mail epm@educ-personnel.co.uk
website: www.epm.co.uk

Institute of Personnel and Development
IPD House
35 Camp Road
London SW19 4UX
Telephone 020 8971 9000 (ask for Enquiry Desk)
Website www.ipd.co.uk (accessible to non-members)

National Association of Governors and Managers (NAGM)
Suite 1, 4th Floor
Western House
Smallbrook Queensway
Birmingham B5 4HQ
Telephone/Fax: 0121 643 5787
E-mail: governorhq@hotmail.com
website: www.nagm.org.uk

National Governors Council
Glebe House
Church Street
Crediton
Devon EX17 2AF
Telephone: 01363 774377
Fax: 01363 776007
E-mail: ngc@ngc.org.uk
website: www.ngc.org.uk

THE EDUCATION PERSONNEL MANAGEMENT SERIES

THE WELL TEACHER
promoting staff health, beating stress and reducing absence

by Maureen Cooper
ISBN: 1-85539-058-2

Gives clear management strategies for promoting staff health, beating stress and reducing staff absence. Stress is not peculiar to staff in education, but is a common cause of absence. Large amounts of limited school budgets are spent each year on sick pay and supply cover. This book gives straightforward practical advice on how to deal strategically with health issues through proactively promoting staff health. It includes suggestions for reducing stress levels in schools. It also outlines how to deal with individual cases of staff absence.

MANAGING POOR PERFORMANCE
handling staff capability issues

by Maureen Cooper and Bev Curtis
ISBN: 1-85539-062-0

This handbook explains clearly why capability is important, and gives advice on how to identify staff with poor performance and how to help them improve. It outlines the legal position and the role of governors, and details the various stages of formal capability procedures and dismissal hearings. The book provides model letters to use and is illustrated by real-life case studies. This provides the help you need to give you confidence in tackling these difficult issues.

Other Network Educational Press Publications

THE SCHOOL EFFECTIVENESS SERIES

Book 1: *Accelerated Learning in the Classroom* by Alistair Smith
Book 2: *Effective Learning Activities* by Chris Dickinson
Book 3: *Effective Heads of Department* by Phil Jones and Nick Sparks
Book 4: *Lessons are for Learning* by Mike Hughes
Book 5: *Effective Learning in Science* by Paul Denley and Keith Bishop
Book 6: *Raising Boys' Achievement* by Jon Pickering
Book 7: *Effective Provision for Able and Talented Children* by Barry Teare
Book 8: *Effective Careers Education & Guidance* by Andrew Edwards and Anthony Barnes
Book 9: *Best Behaviour* by Peter Relf, Rod Hirst, Jan Richardson and Georgina Youdell
Book 10: *The Effective School Governor* by David Marriott
Book 11: *Improving Personal Effectiveness for Managers in Schools* by James Johnson
Book 12: *Making Pupil Data Powerful* by Maggie Pringle and Tony Cobb
Book 13: *Closing the Learning Gap* by Mike Hughes
Book 14: *Getting Started: an Introduction guide for Newly Qualified teachers* by Henry Liebling

THE ACCELERATED LEARNING SERIES
Series Editor: Alistair Smith

Book 1 : *Accelerated Learning in Practice* by Alistair Smith
Book 2 : *The Alps Approach: Accelerated Learning in the Primary School* by Alistair Smith and Nicola Call
Book 3 : *Mapwise: Accelerated Learning Through Visible Thinking* by Oliver Caviglioli and Ian Harris

OTHER PUBLICATIONS

Imagine That... by Stephen Bowkett
Helping with Reading by Anne Butterworth and Angela White
Self Intelligence by Stephen Bowkett
Effective Resources for Able and Talented Children by Barry Teare